REMEMBERING
'I AM'

Remembering 'I AM'

Simple Reminders of Presence

Angela Tucker

© Copyright 2021 Angela Tucker
rememberiam2020@gmail.com

All rights reserved. No part of this book may be reproduced in any form or by any electronic or mechanical means without permission in writing from the copyright holder, except for the purposes of review. Scanning, uploading, and electronic distribution of this book is prohibited.

ISBN: 978-0-6450457-0-3

Editing, Design & Typography
D. Patrick Miller • Fearless Literary Services
www.fearlessbooks.com

TABLE OF CONTENTS

INTRODUCTION
1

PART I
WHAT AM I?
3

PART II
WHAT ARE YOU?
13

PART III
REFLECTIONS & RESPONSES
37

ACKNOWLEDGEMENTS
135

INTRODUCTION

Have you ever been troubled by this feeling: *There must be more to life?*

There was never a great booming voice from above that answered this disturbance for me. Instead I began to experience a gentle, consistent unfolding of new awareness enabling me to distinguish what is *not real*, as well as everything *I am not*. In the peeling away of perceptions that had blinded me and beliefs that imprisoned me, I have begun to recognise and remember who I truly *am*. This recognition told me: *Yes, there is much more.*

The legendary film 'Shawshank Redemption' echoes my learning experience. A falsely imprisoned man obtains a tiny pick, seemingly to sculpt his rock collection and while away the endless time of his sentence. But over many years, he also uses it to chip away secretly at his prison wall, fashioning a narrow tunnel for his eventual escape. One night he silently slips away to freedom.

Maybe I could see the light at the end of my tunnel because I have always felt a calling to dig, dig, dig and not give up. Many distractions have called to me along the way — but that light has been so bright in my awareness that there was never any doubt that something was waiting for me.

2

Over the years I have called this light many names — God, Jesus, Truth, Holy Spirit, Freedom, Love — but the words always limited the reality I felt was calling me. Keeping my attention on this light instead of words or concepts, my habitual perceptions and beliefs were slowly chipped away.

This book is an attempt to share my learning with anyone who has sensed a similar drawing toward the light of self-knowledge. Offering these words to you feels like breaking through the end of my long tunnel, giving myself permission to let go of any remaining judgements or defenses that I might still be tempted to use in order to protect the person I once thought I was.

The book is structured to invite your responses to the thoughts and feelings I have experienced in my process of self-awareness. "I Am" just as "You Are" — and inwardly we are more alike than different. Feel free to respond, or not, as each passage or question is placed before you.

I invite you to to recognise and fall in love with your true self.

PART I

WHAT AM I?

4

I Thought I Was A Body

I had thought I was a body walking around on this earth — a body that was born, had grown and would eventually die. Watching it, I have seen this body go through so many changes. Cell by cell, what was once there no longer exists. The way I have felt about this body and how I have treated it has also changed continuously throughout my life.

The way this body has performed and how I have used its different parts has always been in flux as well. What I experience physically today will change by tomorrow, if not sooner — forever moving, ever changing — a rollercoaster ride of joy and grief.

As I continue to watch my body I recognise that it is not me. My body is definitely something I have and use, but it is not who I am. How could it be, if what is here now is not what was here before, or what will be here in years to come?

Having left behind the idea of being a body I continue to look toward the end of the tunnel, following the light of the truth. I still experience feelings, sensations and ideas about this body, watch it move about and use it to communicate … but I know it is not who I am.

Many Roles

Many roles have been played out by this body during this lifetime. When I was born I was already taking on roles including daughter, sister, grand-daughter, cousin, and niece.

Over the years I grew into many more roles: auntie, student, friend, wife, mother, teacher, and colleague. Some roles have ended and others have arisen over time, like hats put on, worn out, replaced, or sometimes put on again. Having watched myself play these roles I have felt satisfaction at times, guilt at others. I have judged my performances according to the expectations of others as well as my own.

We may inhabit many roles but only play out a few at a time. As these roles have been taken on or ended, I know that none of them are truly permanent, and they are not who I am. I can play them out to the fullest, but they are not me any more than the hats I may put on and take off. How can they be me, if they keep changing?

6

Labels

My country of birth was Australia, so they call me an Australian. My skin colour has been referred to as white, so they say I am a Caucasian. My parents were born in Germany and Israel, so I am referred to as multicultural. If you are born in one country and emigrate to another you can obtain a new title of citizenship and thus change how people refer to you.

If you take on religious beliefs or join churches they may refer to you as Buddhist, Christian, Hindu, Islamic, or even atheist. As I have shared and joined with certain groups, so have I changed how I refer to myself, and how others refer to me. Such labels of belief have included, for me, Methodist, Christian, and Mystic.

Along with the labels I have collected and sometimes discarded, some beliefs and values have come and gone as well. As I have put on and peeled off these labels, I can see that they are secondary to who I am.

If labels can be put on and taken off then they are not permanent. They are not who I am any more than my body and the roles I've played — my labels and beliefs are all made up, and shifting over time.

Another Personality

When I was a young child I remember being extremely shy and very polite. Later on I was described as *bubbly, friendly, abrupt, thoughtful,* and *distant* — to name just a few of the characterizations. These descriptions would depend on my moods, how I was behaving, and whomever I was interacting with. Sometimes I was pleased with how I behaved, other times not so much.

There seems to be a personality attached to me that is continually changing. Sometimes I like what I see and sometimes I cringe as I witness that personality over time. If it is continually changing then it can't be me any more than my body, my labels, or beliefs. My personality is something I just carry around, use and watch.

Talents and Limits

Growing up in a country town far from the ocean or another large body of water, I had limited opportunity to learn to swim. To this day, I have very limited skills in the water. From a young age I demonstrated a talent for drawing and painting. These hobbies were encouraged and my skill levels eventually grew enough so that I could paint and sell my work.

Each of our lives is determined by various opportunities and limitations, dependent on where we were born, to whom, and our evolving circumstances. Natural talents as well as limitations may also emerge during our lifetime, at different stages and in a variable range.

At times I have witnessed the talents of others and wished they were mine.

All my talents have appeared, flowed more strongly or ebbed over time. Watching these changes I know that I am not my talents or limitations any more than I am my body, my labels, my beliefs or my personality. They are all added *to* me — not really me.

Remember

When I remember I can seem to have an experience again, with all the feelings and emotions that it seemed to contain at the time. As I remember, I join again with that moment.

All that I might remember from the past is not with me now unless I look for it and join with it again. Being past, it is not here now. If it is not here now then it cannot be me, as I am here now.

My past is secondary to who I am; it is not here now so it is really not who I am any more than my body, labels, beliefs, personality, talents or limitations.

The Future That Is Never Here

Some of us seem to have huge ambitions, big dreams for the future, while others develop only limited ideas or plans.

Maybe you want to be a famous artist or architect, as I did years ago, or just find your perfect partner, have children and settle down to a quiet life. You may have ambitions to be rich or live a simpler yet happy life. We all have desires, dreams, plans, and preferences for our future.

My plans and ideas of the future have changed constantly through the years, mostly not turning out the way I thought they would. All the energy I put into desiring, planning and worrying about the future was given to something that was not there, did not exist.

Like my past, my future is not here, so it cannot be me any more than my body, labels, beliefs, personality, talents, limitations or past.

Opinions And Beliefs

Over the years I've held many beliefs and opinions which I have collected from others, picked up through reading and learning, and from direct experience.

I have watched my beliefs and opinions develop, change and drop away over the years. Some have helped me through life and others have seemed to either support me to connect to others or withdraw and look for like-minded people.

Picking up, modifying, letting go or replacing indicates that these opinions and beliefs are very unstable, some more so than others. They seem to be optional to my existence in this world.

So how can beliefs or opinions be what I am? They cannot be me any more than my body, labels, beliefs, personality, talents, limitations, past or future.

Just A Thought

My thoughts have been experienced as a continuous flow passing through my mind. Some thoughts hang around for a while, others briefly visit and depart. Some I have had to track down while others seem to haunt or taunt me.

They come and they go, ever moving and never staying indefinitely.

My thoughts are just that — they are MY thoughts, not me. I have found that I can let them come and go, knowing that they are not me any more than my body, labels, beliefs, personality, talents, limitations, past, future, beliefs or opinions. My thoughts don't actually touch or change who I really am.

PART II

WHAT ARE YOU?

By looking at everything I am *not*, I began to glimpse who I truly am, who I have always been.

If you would like to try this path to look for yourself, please read on. Consider each question thoughtfully, page by page, before moving to the next.

14

Can you see that you are not a body? You do seem to have one. You can continue to use your body but for now, just put aside the idea that it's actually what you are.

What are the roles you have been assigned, or taken on? Can you see that you are not any of these roles? They can be put on or taken off. For now, put them aside, outside your idea of yourself.

What are some of the labels that have been attached to you, or that you created for yourself? For now, peel them off and place them outside yourself.

What is your personality like? Can you actually describe or pin it down? Can you see that it's not actually what you are? You have had a personality but it is constantly changing. Set it aside for a few minutes.

What are your talents, and what are their limits? These are capabilities you have but they are not permanent to you. For now let's just set them aside.

Can you see that your past is just that? It has passed and is no longer here, unless you choose to remember and call it back? So let's just leave it outside for now

Can you see that your future is not yet here? It doesn't really exist now, and is present only in thought. Let's drop that thought for now.

21

All the beliefs and opinions which you have collected and lost — including any regarding this book — exist only in your thoughts. Are you willing to put them aside for now?

22

The thoughts that constantly stream through your mind are each here for a moment, then just as quickly gone. Can you see that all the thoughts gone missing are not you?

23

All of the layers of the person that you have collected you can now leave aside for just a few moments...

24

ARE YOU STILL HERE?

HOW DO YOU FEEL?

26

HAVE YOU ALWAYS BEEN HERE?

HAVE YOU EVER REALLY CHANGED?

DO YOU HAVE ALL THAT YOU NEED
RIGHT NOW IN THIS MOMENT?

29

CAN YOU STAY HERE?

30

CAN YOU LIVE FROM HERE?

31

CAN YOU ASK FROM HERE?

32

CAN YOU LISTEN FROM HERE?

I INVITE YOU TO STAY HERE AND LET YOUR
LIFE UNFOLD NATURALLY.

34

YOU ARE REAL.

YOUR LAYERS MAY CALL YOU BACK, BUT YOU NEED NOT LOSE YOURSELF IN THEM AGAIN.

YOU CANNOT PERFECT YOUR PERSON,
BUT YOU CAN DROP YOUR PERSON
IN ORDER TO SEE YOUR
TRUE PERFECTION.

PART III

REFLECTIONS & RESPONSES

As I recognise who I am and see where I am, everything else falls away and the love story of my real life is revealed. Created by Love and carried by Love, my life continues to unfold. Words can only attempt to describe what sustains me; whether I say God, Love, Source or Truth, it's all the same to me.

The following pages are extracts from my journal writings.
I can only share what I experience, not to preach or teach, but only to extend and point to the Love that seems to flow through me. The words I use may be my limitations, my cages, as Truth has no words. So I invite you to reflect on your own experience between these passages and between my words, so that you may sink into your own knowing to find your own answers.

May you recognise the home you never left and live from here.

My Thoughts

My thoughts are like waves in the ocean of life
I give my all to you
I release my thoughts into your depths
That I may settle in your stillness
And know you — be with you

My thoughts are like clouds in the vastness of life
I give them all to you
And watch them float by, disappearing as a puff of wind
What remains is and always has been
Your eternal being
My life is in you — always.

No need to follow the story
Or remember the words or pictures
Just the knowing
Of the Storyteller

This is how I remember that my thoughts are not me. Without them I am still knowing the Storyteller without the story — how about you?

Miracle

You always answered me when I asked you
'What is a miracle?"

I always heard you say
"You are!"

But I never quite realised what you meant
Now I do

I am the miracle you are unfolding,
the flower you are blooming

There is nothing I need do
But watch and be in awe

Of your majesty and power
Of your love and perfection

In knowing your creation
And sharing this with me

You are my Maker — I am your miracle

Finally I recognized that I am a miracle, perfectly made by my Maker.
Do you know your Maker and see that your being is a miracle?

Calling for Love

My thoughts
Are either of love or a call for love
Nothing to fear

My words
Are either of love or a call for love
Nothing to fear

My actions
Are either of love or a call for love
Nothing to fear

I see only love or a call for love
I see me

In recognising this, now I see only expressions of Love. What do you see?

Hide and Seek

I can only know LOVE
    Because that is what I am
Fear is merely the forgetting of who I am

I can only know JOY
    Because that is what I am
Sorrow is merely the forgetting of who I am

I can only know PEACE & REST
    Because that is what I am
Unrest is merely the forgetting of who I am

I can only know ONENESS
    Because that is what I am
Seeing an "other" is merely the forgetting of who I am

I can only BE awareness
    Because that is what I am
Doing is the forgetting of who I am

I can only know YOU and BE me

And yet
I play
Hide and Seek
with YOU

I seem to really know myself, my true essence, only when I am not hiding in my story. Are you hiding or are you recognising your true self?

Dear Mind

Dearest Mind,

> I am here now
> Peace is here now
> Love is here now
> Joy is here now

So
Rest in me

My mind is something I have and so I invite it to rest in me. Are you also able to call your mind to rest in your presence?

Unlimited Potential

Life cannot be contained
This world, this experience is IN ME.
My dreams appear IN ME
This life, this person appears IN ME
My thoughts are IN ME
This world of perceptions are but thoughts IN ME
My mind is IN ME
Come rest mind, IN ME, as I rest IN GOD
Time and space are IN ME, in my awareness, my spirit
I am the awareness and my perceptions are my play
I am unlimited potential

From my point of view there seems to be no limits to what could unfold in my experience. Could there be any limits to you experiencing your potential?

Osmosis

Osmosis of Life
I am one with God,
like a drop in the ocean,
fully alive and flowing,
no beginning, no end, eternal.
Knowing God in stillness and playing the game of life in awareness,
always conscious, here, now.

My life seems to be flowing through all that I know here and now.
Where is your life flowing?

In This Moment

I enjoy this moment: I am Joy
I love this moment: I am Love
I am at peace in this moment: I am Peace

As a movie can be enjoyed including the sad, scary, confusing parts,
From the safety and comfort of my chair

So life can also be enjoyed in its fullness
From the safety and comfort of my home within

When I watch my story I can remember where I am watching from, or I can get distracted and lost in what's happening. Can you watch your story from your place of knowing — your home?

Makes No Difference

What I see and experience
  Makes no difference

What I do and say
  Makes no difference

What I feel and think
  Makes no difference

What I believe and understand
  Makes no difference

What I remember and forget
  Makes no difference

To who I am

Enjoy and trust — all is well.

My true essence has never been affected by any experience. Are you still the same you that you always have been?

Sunrise

As I sit and attempt to watch the sunrise, I am drawn to notice
There is a soft gentleness in this phenomenon.
From darkness to light, the change appears
But I cannot perceive the movement of change.
So gentle, no movement can be seen
Yet blackness becomes shades of grey, then shades of blue.
As I continue to watch, a soft pink haze is seen.
If I look away to write and then look again, the soft pink is now a vibrant hot pink.
Shapes and forms in my garden and beyond have come into being, becoming clearer and lighter.
No matter how intensely I look, this movement of light I cannot see, yet, all is changing.
Is this I,
my light of being,
changing this world,
so gently that I am not aware,
not yet?

My mind tells me that there is change and movement, yet I cannot see either; I can only see now. Is anything changing or moving? Are you changing or moving? Or is your mind just telling you a story?

Seeking nobody

Deep sleep where are you?
My only place of perfect, complete peace.
Why do I look for you?
My resting place where I know all is well and I am all,
    complete and at peace.
As I dream, many experiences unfold and thoughts are abounding.
When I awake, the experiences and thoughts continue to unfold.
In waking, and in dreaming I seek for rest and peace.
Teach me to know this perfect rest and peace
As I walk in these worlds.
Teach me to accept and enjoy all states
As the unfolding reveals who I am, where I am, when I am.
I am here, now, all is well
Help me to be nobody.

The only experience that relieves me of being a person is what I enjoy most: deep sleep. What state do you enjoy the most — waking? dreaming? deep sleep? Why?

Enjoying Love

Can I enjoy
    Every thought that flows through me?
Can I enjoy
    All sights that appear in me?
Can I enjoy
    Every sound, all words that echo in me?
Can I enjoy
    Each sensation that vibrates in me?
Can I enjoy
    The emotions that rise and fall in me?
As my attention
    Sinks deep into my being
    Becoming ever rooted in you
Yes
Thoughts are cries for Love
Sights are reflections of Love
Sounds are echoes of Love
Sensations are vibrations of Love
Emotions are pulsations of Love
    All is Love
        All is One

Without labelling my experiences I can see that I am free to enjoy them all when I cease to judge them. Can you enjoy all of your experiences this way?

The Movies

When I walk out of our local cinema the person at the door always asks 'Did you enjoy the movie?'
I usually answer 'Yes, thank you'
It doesn't matter if the movie was funny, scary, sad or twisted, no matter which characters there were, what emotions they brought out, or what thoughts they provoked.
Whatever experiences I had in that cinema, I knew it was just a movie to enjoy.
I knew that I walked out the same as I walked in — nothing in that movie had changed who I am.
So is life.
May I enjoy each scene, each moment, each character — knowing that the script is written, the movie is complete and I am still as God created me.
May I not forget this.

There have been many movies I have enjoyed and it seems that the more intense they are, the more my enjoyment. Do you enjoy scary movies? Tear jerker movies? Action movies? Tragedies and dramas? Why not enjoy the same experiences in life?

In Laughter

Why on earth would I get upset about something I can't change? This I who gets upset or even slightly irritated cannot change anything and does not really exist.
In laughter, I can see this truth.
All is well

Can you see this and laugh?

The True Teacher

A true Teacher in this world of symbols only points to the truth of where I am already.

Can you see that your true Teacher is within you, not out there?

Leaving Tracks

As I walked today I was drawn to the tracks on the dirt road — impressions left by animals, cars and bikes.

As I looked across the paddocks I saw impressions and tracks from tractors, headers and probably critters if I looked more closely. As my eyes headed to the ocean I saw the white caps of the waves rolling across the sea.

The impressions on the road and in the paddocks last for a while, but were fading and would soon be gone. The waves in the ocean leave no such impressions, they last but an instant and are gone.

May I be like ocean.

Tracks can tell a story and draw one's attention away from where you are. Don't follow my tracks. Can you see that you are always where you are meant to be?

Robot Dream

Waking from a dream this morning:
I was in a car with others and we had an accident which sent us over a dirt rise and off the edge of a huge cliff. As we were falling to our death we each looked at the other and I said *I love you* to each other and knew all would be ok, all would be revealed.
We all awoke in this other world, no longer as people in a movie world but now like robots, almost animated, robots that had been built to mimic people. I thought, *God please don't let it be true that I am really a robot and nothing more*. Then this giant claw came out and one by one collected all the robots including all my friends, but I was left.

When I was spotted they said 'There she is' and took me aside. I was quite distressed about my friends and what would happen to them and to me - I wanted to save them. They tried to explain to me that I was not what I thought and that I had done something to myself so I could not understand. They took out a small device and said 'Why did you turn this off?' I didn't know what is was, hadn't seen it before, but they told me it was mine and that I had taken it with me into a world that I had chosen to live in. It would have kept me connected to them, to know it was not real, just a game I was playing. This seemed to make sense but I couldn't know for sure. Then they switched it back on. Immediately I sensed this in my mind and I knew that it was all true. I had chosen to go into that new world but I had also at some point chosen to turn off the device, the knowing. I had grown such a love for the robots that I still wanted to save them, even knowing they were not real like me.
Is the device on now — can I see?

My dreams speak to me in symbols that help me to question all that I perceive. How do your dreams speak to you?

Learning to Float

Learning to float — to trust.
I am the awareness of this world, the awareness of my perceptions, my experiences unfolding.
As I learn to trust, to float, I can see that existence is like the ocean — fluid, ever moving and changing. It is my mind's madness to think I can know anything, control anything, do anything. I cannot control existence, I can only experience its unfolding.
Past, present, future, time, space are all moving, changing concepts that are projections from the place I am watching from.
As I rest and trust, I see.
If I try, if I think, I am blinded.
All is unveiled as I rest in you.
That last two percent, the last step, is by Grace alone, by trusting and letting go.
Now is Salvation,
Peace, Love, Joy, Understanding
Knowing God.

Trust was a huge barrier for me for some time and only gradually emerged as the layers of self-defense dissolved. Whom do you trust? Do you trust yourself enough to let go of control? Why not give it a try?

Breathing

As I breathe, life moves from my home to flow into this world.
As I follow my breath, I remember my home. The energy that flows in this breath is the love, peace and joy that I breathe into this shadowland, moment by moment, breath by breath.
Like a deep sea diver or an astronaut in space — my life line to home is always in place.
I know of my home in each breath.

Simply following my breath helps to keep me in this moment. You can try this too — any time, any place — and see what you discover.

Seeing

Through all my activity and the experience of my senses, the light of my home shines into this shadowland, creating a world of illusions, reflections of home.
The light of truth, of love shines forth through my sight, my hearing, all sensing and feeling.
My awareness is my connection to my home, to remember where I am.
My experiencing is the evidence of my life.
I am alive, life.
The fine tuning is by Grace.

Seeing my eyes as projectors has helped me look within for the Source of life. Where does your seeing come from?

Body

My body is an instrument, a communication device,
a bridge to reach the divine,
a channel for love, peace and joy to pass through.
For sharing, for the gift of giving life,
for play and enjoyment,
for accepting and connecting that which is already one.
Interacting in this world,
part of this world, not separate.
Absorbing light, air, water, food,
eventually given back to the earth,
taking in breath from the plants, trees and
giving back breath, life.

How do you see your body?

All is well

Now is the only place I can see clearly, all else does not exist. There is no sense in trying to see past or future with an insane mind. No sense in trying to sort thoughts or plan ideas; all that is futile.
Now all is well, all is perfect, all is calm.
The gift of peace is always available, now, all is well.

As I recognise now there is nothing else. Do you recognise your peace in this moment? Do you feel the comfort here?

Journey

Believing is still the journey
    that does not exist,
        the play of illusionary life.

Knowing is being home:
    the truth,
    reality of life,

Found only in this moment.

Finding that there is nothing to believe in, I am free to know life fully. Do you hold onto any beliefs that are holding you back from knowing truth? See what happens if you let them go.

Clouds

Some clouds that pass by are more noticeable than others, catching my attention.
But they are still clouds,
    passing, soon to disappear.
        This is Grace
        This is Life
My attention will not stop them
    from fading into nothingness

Nothing I have tried to hold onto has lasted, all has faded. Have you noticed any appearances in your life that remain? Look closely.

Mirror

I am responsible for the world I see and for the people I meet.
I will not perceive a healed world until I know my true self and live
and respond as my true self.
This world is a reflection, a mirror of who I think I am.
When I know, when I remember who I truly am,
then I can be my true self
and the world will reflect this truth.

If what I perceive is a reflection of what I think then change can only come from within. As I take all discomfort to my Source I find the answers there. I invite you to take all your questions there and see what you uncover. (If I see a dirty mark on my face in a mirror, I don't wipe the mirror, I wipe myself!)

Changing Channels

As I awoke this morning I had a strong impression that the channel abruptly changed on the screen.
As the dream ended, another story began.
I am the screen, the awareness.
Dreams are the stories that play out, night dreams, day dreams, deep sleep all play out before me.
As the awareness of them all, I do not change.
Nothing can touch me.
I watch and learn that
I am nothing.

Seeing that through all my states of awareness I seem to remain just me helps me to let all things be. What do you find for yourself?

Silence

In the night
I sense the power
The power of silence.
There is strength and wisdom
    as well as peace and protection
        in Silence,
            where I abide.

Sound doesn't seem possible without silence, and I have learnt to love my place of silence. Do you constantly seek for sound to cover over your silence or are you able to enjoy it?

Game or Puzzle

If life is a game, then I would be playing to win.
If I intend to win, then there must be someone who loses.
To be right is to make another wrong.
To win is to make another lose.
    But there is no other!

If life is a puzzle then I intend to solve it.
The creator of a puzzle intends the player to solve their puzzle;
    there is no loser here.

If God is Creator of life, then I am.
If a puzzle is to be solved, then I am.
I am both puzzle and solution,
    I am.
Knowing there is no duality, only one,
    I am.
Knowing the illusion and play of life,
    I am.
Being, experiencing and knowing,
    I am.
Peace, Love and Joy in acceptance of what is,
    I am.

No more battling to win a game, now just the enjoyment of the puzzle that appears as my story. Do you battle life as a game or can you accept and enjoy life as a puzzle to solve?

Safe

There is nothing to protect
There is no one to protect
Protection is the mind's activity, attempting to control the illusion.
Protection is a form of judgement, measuring and choosing what the mind considers best or good.
There is, in truth, no good or bad, no need of judgement.
Forgiveness and acceptance is the way of truth.
No need to protect — I am safe
All is One, is Safe.

In recognising where I eternally abide, I see that my safety is secure. Do you see your true self as safe? Is there really anything that can touch this?

Joy

I asked: Where is the Joy?

As I walked, putting aside any thoughts on where to go, I had three encounters.

First I met two people I know, my cousin and his wife, whom I had not spoken to for many years. They told me about their trip to China next week and it was a fun encounter. As I left I told them to enjoy their trip.

Second, I met an older woman on my path who wore serious walking shoes and carried two walking sticks. I told her that she looked like she was seriously walking and she told me she had walked 18 kilometres with four to go, and where she had come from. As I walked on I told her to enjoy her walk.

Third, I came across a younger woman happily walking her dog. I told her how happy her dog looked and she told me how excited he was as he was pulling her along on the lead. I told her to enjoy him while she can.

As I walked on I heard you say 'See! You are the Joy' and tears of gratitude fell down my cheeks. Remembering that if I feel I am lacking anything at all, I need only to give it away to see that it was within me all along.

I offer joy to this world, as my joy is abundant in God.

When I think that anything is missing I have learnt to ask within, and the answers appear either in words or events like this these. If you feel anything is missing, such as your joy or peace… why not ask and then be open for the answers?

Understanding

Understanding takes no time, is timeless.
Thinking is in time but when the understanding is recognized, thinking is cleared, disappearing like clouds into a timeless Awareness.

*Have you ever had **ah ha!** moments when you just 'get it'? Where does that come from?*

River

As a river
   the love, peace and happiness
      that I am
         flows freely into this perceived world
Only thoughts and perceptions
   of a separate mind and body
      appear to block or inhibit
         this freely flowing river of life
Setting aside thoughts and perceptions
   of a personal self
      these blocks soon appear
         only as waves, as currents
            settling to ripples
               before sinking into stillness
The stillness and silence
   that allows
      the river to gush and flow
         freely
The person then perceived, not as separate
   but as a channel
      until the channel dissolved
         entirely into being
            One River.

When my thinking subsides I find that my day unfolds naturally and beautifully. What do you find when your thinking subsides? Does this seem more natural and real to you too?

This

I am
I am here
I rest
I play
All thoughts and perceptions
    are my play
No resistance
    is my rest
My stillness and silence
    is ever present — eternal
My acceptance of experience in play
    is infinite
I ponder my self
I let go all concepts of other
I accept
I smile and laugh

Resting in myself provides a much clearer view of a reality which I love.
What do you find when you rest in just being here?

Dreaming

In my dreams last night I was walking along a beach and saw a large bird fall from the sky. As I looked up there were hundreds of these very large birds flying about circling above the one that had fallen. I walked along the beach with my camera photographing the birds. The beach appeared in pastel orange and pink haze and the breaking waves in soft white — all spectacular.

I recall thinking 'Wow, this is so unbelievable what I see and yet I know that this is not a dream, this is real - I am awake and seeing, experiencing all this, I know I am awake!'

How strange now, as I think of this, that I was SO sure I was awake and yet I was dreaming.

But I know I am awake now… Am I?

Or am I still dreaming?

In dreams I usually don't know that I am dreaming, but sometimes I do have lucid dreams and watch myself from my place of sleep. How do you know when you are dreaming?

In this Dream

In this dream, now
    images appear and then are gone
    as I look around
In this dream, now
    sounds are heard but then fade
    as other sounds arise
In this dream, now
    sensations of touch
    heighten then melt away
In this dream, now
    feelings shuffle within me
    seeming to call for attention
In this dream, now
    my thoughts play
    as if being tossed in a game
In this dream, now
    all experiences come and go
    and yet, I know
This is a dream, now

As I see my current experience as a dream, I am able to watch myself experiencing life from the safety of my home, like lucid waking — there seems to be no difference. Are you experiencing lucid waking? Is this all a dream?

As a Diamond

Thank you for reminding me that as a diamond has many facets
    that shine uniquely
so each soul shines your light perfectly.
One diamond, one whole, yet shining in many ways.
As we each have unique perceptions and see different worlds,
our eyes as projectors shine into this world your light:
unique and perfect.

I know I have a unique view of this world, but are we just like one diamond shining as many facets?

The Only One

I am the only one who sees
    as I see
I am the only one who hears
    as I hear
I am the only one who feels
    as I feel
I am the only one who smells
    as I smell
I am the only one who thinks
    as I think
I am the only one who knows
    as I know
I am the only one who remembers
    as I remember
I am the only one who lives
    this life
I am this life's source
    that shines
I am as You created me
    to Be

My experiences are unique to me, flowing from me, from my Source.
Where do your experiences come from?

No Grievances

Love holds no grievances
I hold no grievances
When I let my grievances go, I know I am perfectly safe

Love holds no grievances
God holds no grievances
Let me not betray myself or my God

Love holds no grievances
I wake to myself, by laying all grievances aside
and waking in Him

All that I see is a reflection of me
Let me hold no grievances
to images I see

All are my Self, all is but one
Accept, Love and be Free
I am Safe, one in God, I rest.

In accepting and letting of everything I think has happened and is happening to me, I have found a beautiful freedom. Are you holding onto any grievances?

The News Reader

I awoke from my dreaming, realising that my mind was busy making stories — mixing up images from my past, my ideas and experiences.

I am awake now, realising that my mind continues making stories, telling tales of past woes and woes to come.

My mind is a storyteller, a newsreader, always trying to get my attention and distract me from the truth.

The truth is that I am free, I am still, I am perfect and in my silence is the peace of God, the love and joy of reality.

As I remember this, I rest, knowing that I am still the peace, love and joy that I was created to be and share.

All thoughts of the past and things to come are merely the echoes of my ego, calling me — but I need not follow. I can remember the truth and stay in my safe abode with You, listening to your soft, still voice directing me, reminding me, loving and encouraging me to stay, rest and learn.

My learning is the remembering of who I am, who I have always been. May I share only your words, your peace, love and happiness. As I share truth into my shadow land, all false images will fade away to reveal the reality of my life.

Each step takes me closer to home, the home that I am already in. Each step opens my eyes and heart to see that I never left, all is well. God directs my every move, my every moment, my every step; as I remember this, so I am FREE.

Like having the news sounding off in the background and letting it be, I have learnt to let my mind play in the background of my awareness and not steal my attention. Can you let your mind tell its stories while you rest in your home? Can you listen to your heart, your soul, rather than your mind?

Alphabet Soup

Life is like a big bowl of alphabet soup.
I can either be grateful and enjoy devouring what is offered
or
I can cause myself grief by trying to make words and meaning out of the letters I find.

The flavour of this world seems to taste the best when I accept each mouthful, each moment without question. How grateful are you for this moment?

Our Song

Our song
> is the song of love
> the song of silence,
> of beauty and peace

This song
> is a perfect orchestra
> of instruments playing all at once
> yet, there is but one music

Our song
> embraces all words
> yet has no words
> but perfect harmony

This song
> cannot be heard
> yet plays out eternally
> calling me home

Our song
> is the celebration of life
> a life that never ends
> but can be forgotten…
but for a moment.

I can see life as a song. The silence between the notes is as important as the sounds. What do you hear when you listen to life?

My Experience

My experience is complete;
    there are no edges, no boundaries.
Sensations arise and disperse
    in my awareness
Perceptions appear and disappear
    in my openness
No part of my experience
    is more mine than another
There are no parts, no mine
    and no other, only one
The forgetting of who I am
    shifts my attention to illusions
Thoughts may arise
    that call for my attention
If followed, these thoughts
    lead me into fantasy:
A story, a fairy tale of
    a limited self that is not real
Tales of suffering and
    tales of pleasure unfold
But I am
    never changed
        never moved
            from being one.

Experiencing seems to be my expression, not separate from me but always expressing me. How do you see experiencing? Where are you without experiencing?

Dreaming

In my dreaming
    I see only myself
    I meet only myself
    I talk only to myself
    I love only myself
    I fear only myself
    I accept only myself

There is no other
    And yet
        I seek Love
        I seek Peace
        I seek Happiness

Who is this that seeks?
    Not me,
        I am here.

Even in my dreams I seem to be searching and yet it is only me present. In your dreams do you imagine and search? When awake, do you imagine and search? Where are you?

Abidance

Abidance is the key
    to remaining aware of love
    my attention on my source

Allowing this world, this
    seeming life story
    to unfold like a flowing river

To trust that God is in control, that
    all which I experience is past
    for my learning, for good

God is the Creator and
    all that He has created
    is good

I am His child, created in
    His image, perfect and holy
    all else is but an illusion

In my dreams I learn of
    who I am not, so that I can
    accept and know who I am

Resting in His truth
    I am home, I am free
    to love, be at peace
        and know joy.

God and Creator are but words, symbols that point to my Source, where I abide. From here I learn what I am not. What words or symbols do you use to point to your source? Where is your home?

Abiding in Source

Looking for answers in the world is looking in the wrong place. Lessons taught by life are temporary, fleeting and unreliable. True learning comes only from Truth, from Spirit, from the stillness and silence of my home, from God.

As I abide in my source, the dance of life unfolds and vibrates before me. Attentive to your words I rest under your protective wings. Thoughts, feelings and sensations flow freely through a heart that forgives, allowing life to tell its story.

The script is written and the story is done, nothing to control or do. In celebration I rest.

A world that calls for my attention only receives my acceptance, love, peace and happiness.

No beginning and no end in reality and yet the seeming story continues but all is for good and the ending is happiness.
So why wait? happiness is now
        as I accept and BE in LOVE

Now I take all my questions within, to my Source, and there I find all my answers. Do you take your questions to the world or within? Can you hear your answers from within? Where is your trust?

Mind Plays

As my mind sleeps,
    I am safe, at home, in my bed of bliss.

As my mind plays in the backyard,
    it is aware of its home and enjoys its adventures, close and safe.

As my mind plays in the front yard,
    still aware of home, knowing that parents are close,
    watching lovingly, as mind imagines and plays.

As my mind plays, its attention is drawn to outside the front gate,
    tempted by images and imaginings.

As my mind wanders off,
    it is overwhelmed and soon forgets home. Lost and alone it
    stumbles through many adventures. Signs and symbols soon
    appear to remind it of home and it begins to seek.

My mind searches for home. Yet I never left.

When you watch your mind play, what do you see? Where is your mind now?

A Parent's Heart

I will always love you
    no matter how your appear to me
I will always love you
    no matter what you say or do
I will always love you
    no matter what you think of me
I have always loved you
    before your birth and after death
I have always loved you
    this love can never cease
In my heart you will always be
    my one and only holy child
My love for you is true and eternal
    flowing from the love I receive
    from my Father
As I am loved, so I can love.

Having a child and being a child in this world has opened my heart to see and know the love that I was created in is to share. Where does the love that you share come from? Do you really know and accept this love?

River of Life

Sweet, sweet river of life
    I watch you flow through me
The light of my awareness
    illuminates your beauty
You take my breath away
    with your vastness and majesty
As I watch your currents flow
    sensations arise and subside
Your aromas call back
    a drawing of breath to enjoy
The tingling vibrations
    dance within me as unending play
Your song is a symphony
    of glorious sounds that tickle
As I dare to taste of your offerings
    the sweetness penetrates my mind
With grace abounding
    I can only accept and enjoy
The gifts you offer
    within this moment
As you reflect within me
    what is: life

As my attention softens I can see life flowing through me. If you open your attention to the vastness of life, without focusing on objects, what do you find?

Free to Love

God is in control
Truth is in control
Let all things be
Let all happenings happen
Accept all experiences
Be grateful and welcoming
Love because that is all that truly exists
Love is truth
Love is God
I am free to love

I love the freedom of being able to love no matter what unfolds. Can you see the freedom in allowing love to flow through you?

One Mind

My beliefs are my limitations
What I believe holds me captive
Not me, but the manifested person that I have created
This person — it seems to exist
Yet, as I look closely, it is not there
Let the character play hide and seek:
Hiding from God, seeking God
These words may appear to be the ravings of a crazed mind
Yes, this mind is crazed
Only the mind of God is sound, is sane
Yet I have the mind of Christ: one mind

No longer trusting an insane mind that holds onto beliefs, I rest in the source of intelligence itself. Do you trust what your mind tells you? Do you hear the truth within, from your Source?

Intensity

As a warm leg stops into the cold waters,
    The intensity is felt
    A reminder
The intensity of light can only be known
    In the darkest of dark
The intensity of comfort can only be felt
    In the midst of pain
The intensity of joy can only be known
    In the depths of despair
The intensity of love can only be felt
    In the loneliness of rejection
From the lowest point in this perceived story
    I cried out to you
There you answered me
    With the intensity of your love and acceptance
This light was your gift to me
    I accepted in gratefulness
May I always remember this
    And shine for you

From sleep to waking there is an intensity, a door
    That allows me to know, to see
    To understand

After questioning all experience, this is my answer. May I encourage you to let go of all concepts and question all your experiencing. Allow the answers to unfold from within, from your silence.

Playpen

This world
    Is my play pen
As I play and explore
    My surroundings
God watches over me
    Protecting and loving me
As I play and experience
    All these sensations
God watches over me
    Guiding and directing me
As I play and pretend
    I am a person creating
God watches over me
    Reminding me who I am
As I play and seek
    His face in other people
God watches over me
    Whispering 'I love you'
As I play and soon
    Begin to tire of life
God waits for me to sleep
    As He opens His arms
        To receive His child
            Who never left Him

In learning that all of my life can be enjoyed when I trust, then in innocence I play and in sleep I rest. How do you see your play of life? Are you playing innocently and resting in His arms?

Ocean

I am as ocean
    A sea of endless potentiality
Ebbing and flowing
    Yet never changing or moving
Attention forms and shifts
    Creating seeming forms
As the experiencer
    I play and learn
As my true self
    I rest in peace and love
In the depths I am
    Free of experience
In the shallows
    I frolic and play
On the surface
    I seem to be tossed, broken
Yet I am
One with you
As ocean
Always

Seeing myself as ocean I can watch the movements of experiencing yet never change my being. Are you one as ocean? What do you see?

The Apple

The apple was meaningless
The tree was meaningless
This world is meaningless
Guilt covered over Love
Giving birth to Fear
Fear is not real
Only the hiding from God
The hiding from Love
Hiding in a world that seems
To separate me from you
Yet I am not separate
I am loved
I am innocent
I am free
To be ME

No more guilt and hiding for me. Are you hiding from Love behind a veil of guilt? Are you telling yourself a meaningless story? Look and see.

Source

I feel you here
    With me, in me, as me
The sensation of life vibrating
    With me, in me, as me
As I play in experiencing, knowing you are
    With me, in me, as me
I am living
    With you, in you, as you
As life's story unfolds, I am still and silent
    With you, in you
As I rest in knowing
    I am with you
As I remember
    I am

There is no separation between me and my Source — we are as one. Do you sense your Source? Know your Source? Live as one with your Source?

Gratitude

Without the pangs of hunger
    A satisfied belly would not be enjoyed
Without the discomfort of the cold
    The warmth of a blanket would not be enjoyed
Without the puzzles of life
    The enjoyment of solutions would not be apparent
Without hiding from you
    The joy of you finding me
        Would not be complete
I play
Hide and seek

My gratitude expands to all my experiencing, knowing all is for good. Do you trust that all experience is ultimately for your good? Can you be grateful for all that seems to unfold for you?

Voice

There is a voice that
    Speaks to you
    All day long
Be still and listen
    To this voice
    From within
Ask your questions
    From here
Listen for answers
    From here
Rest and watch life unfold
    From here

A voice speaks to me from within but is only heard when my mind is silent. What voice do you hear when your world is silent? Have you learnt to trust this voice above all others?

The Tree

As I sit on the roots of this
    Massive fig tree
I can see myself blending
    Like osmosis into its form
My arms reach out and
    Form into new branches
My legs melt deeply
    As roots into the soil
I am as Wisdom
    One with this tree
I offer shade, safety
    And shelter to all
I do not move, no searching
    And no striving
As I grow stronger and
    Wiser, I know
That you are the cause
    Of my being
I am aware of a world
    Moving and changing
From my point of view
    I sit and TRUST

As I recognise the oneness of a tree with its environment, I recognise my oneness with existence. Nourishment and wisdom come naturally when I sit and trust. Where do you see your nourishment coming from? Where does wisdom come from? Where do you sit?

Knowing Myself

I am
    Prior to any experiencing
        That arises in me
I am
    After any experiencing
        Subsides in me
I am
    Knowing all experiencing
        That moves through me
I am
    Unmoved, unchanged
        Accepting of all experience
I am

I am still as God created me — nothing has changed. Have you ever really changed? Are you still the same you? Can anything change this?

Here

I am seeing
    Here, now
I am hearing
    Here, now
I am sensing
    Here, now
I am thinking
    Here, now
I am experiencing
    Here, now
I am peaceful
    Here, now
I am resting
    Here, now
I am aware
    That I am
        Here, now
            Awake

When my mind wanders, calling for attention, these reminders are helpful. Are you here, now? Aware here, now?

Breathing

Experiencing is like breathing
    A natural expression
        Of life, of myself

When I try to control or even watch
    My breath, it becomes
        Stifled, unnatural and difficult

So with experiencing
    I need only let it flow
        Naturally, carefree like
            The Artist's brush

My breathing is such a beautiful reminder of the flow of life. What does your breathing teach you? How do you feel when you let life flow?

Once Upon a Time

Once upon a time
    The wind against my skin
    Seemed to cause me
    Torment and agitation
Once upon a time
    The thoughts arising in mind
    Seemed to cause me
    Anxiety and worry
Now
    The wind against my skin
    Is a caress
Now
    The thoughts arising in mind
    Are gifts to enjoy
Acceptance
    Is liberation
    Is freedom
        To enjoy life

Many things that previously irritated me I can now enjoy. Is there anything that still irritates you? Can you accept and enjoy all of life instead?

Alfa

I am Alfa
    I play
    I have no agenda
    I have no preferences
    I play
I am Alfa
    I am here
    I am now
    My attention swims
    I play
I am Alfa
    This dream is in me
    I dream in day
    I dream in night
    I rest in you
I am Alfa
    In you I exist
    You hold me safe
    My being is pure
    Created in you
I am Alfa
    Angie is my dream

Playfully naming my awareness as Alfa has helped me to watch the story of Angie unfold. What would you name your awareness? Why not play?

Only Me

There is no thinker of thoughts
There is no doer of deeds
There is no planner of life
There is no person to judge
There is only
    Myself, here, now, being
    Light, love and peace

When I look, I find that there is no one doing anything, yet I am here. What do you find when you look closely?

Am I Aware?

From this place
    I am aware
From this place
    I am myself
From this place
    I am

My attention reaches out
    To form this world
    To form this character
    To form dreams

Sinking deep, relaxing my attention
    I am home
    I am free
    I am myself
    I know

As I live from my being I allow
    This story to unfold
    This moment to happen
    This instant to be

From my being
    I know what is
    I know truth
    I am in Love

Remembering where I look from is the awareness that I am. Are you aware? Where do you go to get your answers? Can you stay there?

Fruit

Picking up a piece of fruit

It looks like an apple
It feels like an orange
It smells like a banana
It tastes like a pear
      But it sounds like a pomegranate
What is it?
    I sense it is
        Whatever I choose
            Nothing, I think
                Just a dream

Having attached so many labels and descriptions to all I experience, I can now undo them all and see what is left. If you peel off the labels of your experience what do you find?

Father

Father is lovingly telling me
    A bedtime story
Safe and warm on his lap
    Wrapped in His arms
He whispers softly this
    Magical story of love
So magical are His words
    That I soon forget who I am
Transported into His magical world
    I become a character
The story unfolds around me
    Seemingly a world of form
Aware of His presence and
    Unending love, I know
That the story will be so
    Perfect and ending divine
So I settle down and rest
    Letting Him speak
Attentive to His voice I learn
    The lessons of life
Trusting in His words I enjoy
    This story of LOVE

I do hear an inner voice that I cannot describe, but in this attempt I call Him Father. Is there a voice that speaks to your heart? What is that voice telling you now?

Everyone is Fine

Everyone is fine
    Every point of view
        Every perceived person
            Has created their own illusions
                For their own lessons
                    In their own way
Everyone is fine
    Every character I meet
        Along the road of life
            Is playing their role
                Playing their scene
                    In their own way
Everyone is fine
    From those close to me
        To those in far lands
            All are playing the game
                Fulfilling their roles
                    In their own way
Everyone is fine
    I can visit and see
        From their point of view
            Many visions and sounds
                That point to you

Everyone is fine

My point of view is unique and limited to my experience. I cannot see any other point of view except my own. What do you see?

Now

All time is now
    Nothing is lost
    Nothing is broken
    Nothing is wrong

All time is now
    Memories are ghosts
    Visions are desires
    Desires are dreams

All time Is now
    Nothing is real
    All things experienced
    All is but one

All time is now
    Freedom is now
    Peace is now
    Love never ceased

All time is now
    It is finished
    It is done
    Enjoy and see

Without thinking, I do not experience time. Without your thoughts are you timeless?

Sacred

The sacredness of life
    Surrounds me
    Envelops me
    Penetrates my being

As mind expands to the stars
    So creation extends
    Reaching out
    Forming life eternal

As mind extends to uncover
    That which forms atoms
    Looking smaller and smaller
    New worlds appear

From here, where I am
    Life dances around me
    All experience surrounds me
    Sensations astound me

The vibrations of being
    Have no boundaries
    No beginning, no end
    No parts or pieces

All is one
All is life
All is love

To me, the source of Creation, no matter what the label, is the sacredness of all and all is therefore sacred to me. What is sacred to you?

Seek and You Shall Find

Seek for stars beyond our galaxies
    And you will find more eternal
Seek for pieces within pieces of the particles of matter
    And they will appear unending
Seek for explanations of how things work and behave
    And you will find theories
Seek for meaning within words and the communication of life
    And you will find religions
Seek for a God, a source that guides you
    And you will find a presence
Seek for other than what you are
    And you will find other
Seek to know yourself only
    And you will find yourself
Accept all that is
    And you will find healing
Be all that you are
    And you will find love, one

Some of my seeking and finding cannot be expressed in my limited words. What have you found in your seeking?

Be

I can see more clearly
    When I cease looking with my eyes
I can hear more clearly
    When I stop listening with my ears
I can think much more sanely
    When I stop using my mind
I can feel love's vibration
    When I forget this body
I can know where I am
    When I stop imagining
I can remember who I am
    When all judging ceases
I am free to be me
    When I choose to BE

Being myself, not a story, is where I have found my freedom. Are you free to be without a story?

Escape

Reaching out
    We seek to have
        More and other than this
In illusioned minds
    We gather and collect
        Constructed moments and objects
Attempts to control
    Our collections and stories
        Comparing to others we see
Insanity is born
    As judgments envelope
        Madness tears at the soul
Escape pulls at the heart
    The having holds hostage
        Causing grief and despair
Not having is now sought
    Release from the story
        No more worries
No refuge is found
    In this place or time
        Does death now call?
Deep sleep teases

The more I thought I had, the more I seemed to worry. What do you think you have? What are you afraid to lose?

Experiencing

I am the light
    Experiencing form
I am the silence
    Experiencing sound
I am the one
    Experiencing the many
I am the stillness
    Experiencing the movement
I am the Peace
    Experiencing emotions
I am the Love
    Experiencing sharing
I am complete
    Experiencing brokenness
I dance and play
    Knowing all is well

Nothing I experience is me and yet I am experiencing, so my experience must come from me. Where is your experiencing coming from? Is it arising from you? Where are you?

Searching

I am the truth that I seek by
Searching through my attention
Looking away from myself
    I see only fragments
Reaching out for more
    I find only broken pieces
Desiring fulfilment from other
    I find only fear and unrest
Searching for peace and rest
    I find only sinking ground
Trying to hold onto illusion
    I find only imminent loss
In the letting go and remembering
    Truth sets me free
I am one
    With all that is

Searching for me kept me from finding myself, and letting go set me free. Are you searching for truth? Are you searching for yourself? Or have you let go to find freedom?

Learning

I am
>Where I need to be

I am
>When I need to be

Knowing
>There is no there or then

Aware
>There is only here and now

This here and now
>Is my classroom of life
>>To learn who I am

In dreams day or night
>Many classrooms I visit
>>To learn who I am

Deep sleep is my rest
>My home where I am
>>Loving and knowing

Experience is my learning, which I welcome each day in gratitude. What are you learning in your classroom of life? Can you welcome each day?

Symphony

If each instrument were a
    World, a universe
If each note were a
    Soul, a life
If each gap were a
    Thought, a dream
If the symphony was an
    Unlimited field of potential
The Conductor
    Its source, its intelligence
This note bows
    To the brilliance, the perfection
Of what is
    Perfect harmony

As a note I play my part in the symphony of life. Can you see yourself as a note in this great symphony?

Float

Here I float
    In a sea of possibilities
Here I am
    Overwhelmed by the intimacy
Of my experience
    Sights, sounds, sensations
Manifestations of my soul
    Not only closeness
Oneness
    Each thought arises
Accepted as a reflection
    Of yet another possibility
Past, future, options
    All blending into one
I am here
    Focused in what seems
To be time and space
    Yet this too is only
A shimmer in this
    Eternal ocean of potential
I bow to this moment
    Giving thanks to its Source
I am but one point of view
    Shifting in its glory

Floating is one way in which I can describe my experiencing now. How would you describe your experiencing?

Help Me

Help me to enjoy
    The emerging of the sunrise
Help me to enjoy
    The transforming of a sunset
Help me to enjoy the
    Glorious opening of a flower
Help me to enjoy the
    Formation of a masterpiece

All change celebrates
    The expression of life
May my paintings be enjoyed
    As a taste of this expressing
Each painting unfinished
    As life continuously unfolds
May we all enjoy the journey by
    Unfocusing the destination

What does your heart cry out for? How do you express your heart's desires?

Truth

Watch life
    But don't follow
Listen to life
    But don't believe
See
    The light of Love
Hear
    The word of Truth

The story
    Says look at this, follow me
Truth
    Says look within and Be

Finding truth comes from listening within to understand what is playing before me. Do you follow the play or listen within? Which way brings you peace?

Moving

All is moving
All is in motion
Thoughts drift in and out
Mind is moving
Visions appear then disappear
Sight is moving
Sounds announce and cease
Hearing is moving
Sensations arise then fall
Body is moving
Feelings present and vacate
Attention is moving
Stories awaken in sleep
Consciousness is shifting
I experience all of this
movement in me
I am
    not moving
I am
    here

All movement seems to appear in me, in my stillness. Are you aware of movements in your experience? Are you moving or still?

The Happening

It's happening
    looking around is happening
    a smorgasbord of sights
It's happening
    sounds announcing themselves
    in fluctuations and degrees
It's happening
    movements of a body in
    a changing and shifting world
It's happening
    waves of thought then sensations
    dancing in attention's scope
It's happening
    a continuation of stories
    in waking and in dreaming
It's happening
    this magical play of life
It's happening
    here, where I am
This great happening
    is my life
Nothing is happening
    but me

As I explore what is happening, I find only me. What do you find when you explore your own happening?

Only One

If I was the only one
    who saw the sky as blue
    would I live happily
    under this blue sky?
If I was the only one
    who heard your guiding voice
    would I follow you
    in complete confidence?
If I was the only one
    who could see love
    would I accept each moment
    as a gift?
If I was the only one
    who knew your peace
    would I hold out my hand
    and offer grace?
If I was the only one
    left standing in this world
    would I continue to smile
    and enjoy life?

In questioning myself I reveal my strength to stand alone. What questions can you ask yourself to remember your strength to stand alone?

New World

I choose to see
    a world of
Love expressed in gentleness
Peace poured over all
Joy abounding in vibrance
Abundance shared and not wasted
Creativity celebrated with passion
Kindness reaching the smallest
Calm rolled out unending
Wisdom freely received
Patience not waiting
Knowing the depths of life
Harmony in nature's embrace
Acceptance of what is
Reverence of Source
Freedom to see
    the New World in Order

This is just a play with words to describe possibilities for this world. What words would you play with to describe your perfect world?

Love's Call

Remembering
    When I first heard
        Love's call
Deep within
    A voice penetrated as
        Love's call
In a crowded hall
    I heard His story as
        Love's call
Alone, abandoned and rejected
    I heard His soft whisper as
        Love's call
As I turned to face my Maker'
    I cried out as
        Love's call
Love answered instantly
    in light and knowledge as
        Love's embrace
Now in this place
    I see and hear only
        Love's call

This was my experience as a person when I had given up on my life and finally answered the call I had been hearing throughout life. Can you hear love calling you, and have you answered the call?

Angie

This character
    uses colour
        to express what is unseen
This character
    uses words
        to express inner voices
This character
    uses motion
        to express her desires
This character
    uses thoughts
        to call out for love
This character
    although not real
        expresses love's play
This character
    drifts in and out
        of awareness's realm
This character
    is my expression
        for now

This is how I see Angie, the character I am playing right now, in this play of life. What character do you see yourself playing right now? How would you describe your character? Can you enjoy your character, remembering it is not you?

Fear Not

I do not feel fear
    fear is a label
I do not even feel feelings
    feelings are labels
I experience sensations
    like waves of energy
As I accept these waves
    this story flows freely
When I fight and name
    my experience is suffered
Thoughts tell a story
    of a character at play
Yet I fear not
    only vibrate in love

For me fear is just an illusion, a story my mind tells. Is there anything you fear right now? If you take away the names and labels what is left?

Knowing

When I struggle
    nothing makes sense
    nothing feels right
When I rest
    all thoughts fade
    all sensations soften
Here in your embrace
    I am lovingly held
    I am safe and secure
Here, this is truth
    all is perfect
    all is one
As sleep comes
    so I dream
    so I experience adventure
Yet, in your embrace
    always free
    always knowing
This is life
    who I am
    knowingly

I know the embrace of my Source is eternal and perfect when I trust and rest. Do you know where you are and what holds you? Have you let go of your story's struggles and found your rest?

Lighthouse

I am as a lighthouse
    shining brightly
As light stretching out
    illuminating my story
As house standing still
    my security and home
Waves crash upon my shore
    threatening and teasing
Skies above shift and change
    night twinkles, day dawns
Here I stand firm
    on rock, solid ground
The light, my attention
    shifting in life's play
The eye of my being
    focused beyond
Yet the Lighthouse Keeper
    tends to my lens
Knowing His caring touch
    always at hand
I am a lighthouse
    on solid ground

This is my reflection of the light of awareness illuminating a story while my Source lovingly cares for me. Who tends to you while your story plays out?

If

If counting determines
   how I feel and behave
   then I am bound by numbers
   there is no freedom there
If measuring determines
   how I respond and feel
   then I am bound by measurements
   there is no freedom there
If preferences determine
   how I choose and feel
   then I am bound by preferences
   there is no freedom there
If appearances determine
   how I move and feel
   then I am bound by appearances
   there is no freedom there
If labels and names determine
   how I act and feel
   then I am bound by these
   there is no freedom there
If thoughts determine
   how I feel
   then I am bound by thoughts
     there is no freedom there
Am I bound by anything there?
Or am I free from everything here?
I am not bound there
I am free here

In remembering that I am still HERE, whatever situation I perceive myself to be in, I recognise my freedom. What situations do you see your character playing in? Do you recognise your freedom is here, now?

For Me

For me
the lessons are not in any
events or happenings
that may play out
in this turbulent story

For me
the lessons are in all
the quiet moments
that speak in stillness
in my haven of rest

Here I learn, I am

All the lessons, inspirations and revelations for my character have been found in my quiet rest, not in my story. Where have you found yours? Where does your attention go?

Song of Birds

Listening to morning sounds
    the song of birds
    chattering and twittering
    what do they say?
Are they telling
    stories of past adventures?
Are they sharing
    their plans for the future?
Are they analysing
    their surroundings?
Or are they just
    enjoying their day?
Listening to morning sounds
    the songs of birds
    singing so happily
    nothing to say
But thank you, I love you, enjoy your day!

Many mornings I have enjoyed these sounds in the simplicity of the moment. What does the song of birds say to you?

Waking

I wake
Here I am
Surroundings appear
    images of shapes and colours
As I look around
    names and descriptions come
As the words form
    the thoughts arise
Each named object
    having a story to tell
As body sensations awake
    then memories call out
This character now
    having its own story to tell
Feelings soon follow
    as flavours to choose
The adventure begins
    which way to follow?
Reach out to explore blindly
    or sink within to rest knowingly?
At the end of the day
    this body is soon laid down
I sleep

What happens for you at that magical time of waking in the morning?

Stories

Stories are available
    for my attention
Stories seem to play out
    all around me
Stories seemingly happen
    with or without me
As I rest in my being
    life pauses in silence
There are no stories
    here where I am
Yet, as I stretch out my attention
    the play resumes
From my home, here
    is silence and peace
Knowing this, I know joy
    that cannot be broken
Let the stories play out
    no beginning or end
Just the Love of Life sharing
    no end in sight

From the place of my being I continue to enjoy the play of life. Where is your place of being? Are you able to enjoy all that is from this place? You can read Part II of this book again at any time that may be helpful in remembering who you are.

ACKNOWLEDGEMENTS

I acknowledge the nameless and formless Source of my existence that gracefully called to me through an indescribable voice of Love, and continues to sustain me.

www.ingramcontent.com/pod-product-compliance
Lightning Source LLC
Chambersburg PA
CBHW071404290426
44108CB00014B/1683